A Different Story

by Maya Grant

Illustrated by
Ros Webb
Fashion Illustrator & Artist

Endorsed by
Alana Nichols
Paralympic Gold Medalist

Book design: Anne Thompson, www.ebookannie.com.

Ilustrator: Ros Webb at www.roswebbart.com.

Ordering Information: Special discounts are available on quantity purchases. Contact Marci Grant at bubsmangomedia.com.

Golden/Colorado/ Maya Grant — First Edition

ISBN-13: 978-1548432164

ISBN-10: 1548432164

Printed in the United States of America

This is a **different** story than most 9-year-olds.

me as a Baby

See I was born with
Beckwith Wiedemann Syndrome.
It usually means that one side of your
body is bigger than the other side.

I have a **big** leg ...my right leg is bigger than my left leg.

me having fun

But I don't' let that stop me from **anything**.

When I was born,
my **pancreas** was
bigger than it was
supposed to be.

IT'S A
Girl!

the size of
a babies
↓ thumb

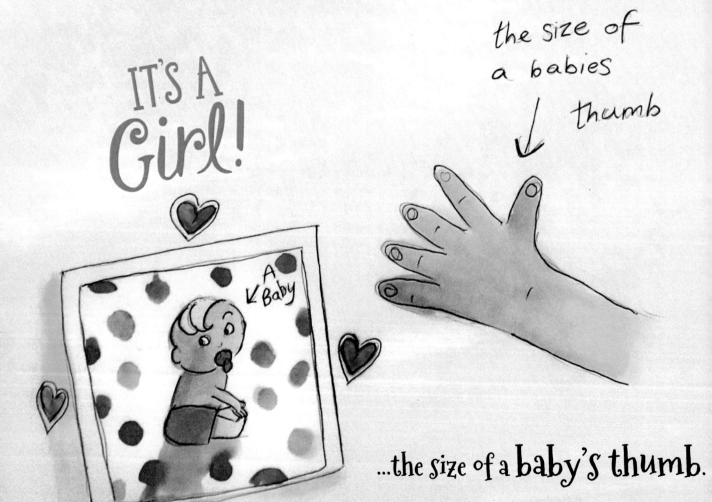

A
Baby

...the size of a **baby's thumb.**

But instead, it was the size of a **man's hand**.
They had to take it **out** and make it the
size it was supposed to be.

↓ MANS HAND ↓

like my
dads
hands

I have had many **surgeries** to help my leg length discrepancy.

When I was about **five years old** I had a surgery.

←me
five
years
old

my
fave
dress →

screws in legs

me playing in the garden

They put **SCREWS** in my bone to slow down the growth of my right leg so my left leg could grow.

When I was about **seven**, I had the screws taken out of my leg.

Because of my leg length discrepancy...
I have to walk on my **tippy toe** on my left leg and on my shoe.

Tippy   Toe

walking on my
tippy toe

We take my shoe to a **Special Doctor** who puts a lift on my shoe to keep my left foot even with my right foot.

Special shoe

I like this style

Having a difference can be a **challenge**.
Lots of people don't know how hard it is to have a **difference**.

Sometimes people tease me because of my big leg.

But the people who tease me are BULLY'S.

Sometimes you can feel **sad** or **mad** because of your difference.

me
happy →

But don't feel sad because there are many people
with differences like YOU and ME.

Don't let your difference BOSS you around.

Don't let **anybody** think less of you because of your difference.

Be YOURSELF
be the person
YOU want to be.

Endorsement

Alana Nichols

THE DAY I MET MAYA was special for a lot of reasons but extra life altering after spending the day on the beach together. I was helping out and coaching at the Challenged Athletes Foundation, Junior Seau Adaptive Kids Camp. When I saw Maya and her Mom walking by, I noticed her big leg. My first thought was, "Wow, she looks athletic! I want to talk to her!" Since I'm paralyzed and was sitting on a blanket in the sand, I couldn't get up to approach Maya so I yelled over to her to come say "Hi." She and her sweet-hearted Mom came over. I asked what adaptive sports she does. She explained that she had never done "adaptive sports" but loved being active!

I talked to her about what I do as a Paralympic athlete and explained why I was at the beach with all these kids with disabilities. We love to surf! I can imagine that word "disability" impacted her in an interesting way. Maybe it was abrasive and unfamiliar at first. We continued to talk about how she felt about her big leg and how sometimes kids her age would treat her differently because of the way she looked. I was moved by her honesty and her Mom's loving encouragement for her to express herself. We both acknowledged how hard it is to be different sometimes. We shared stories of our hardships but by the end of the conversation, I suggested that we start calling her "big leg" her "super leg." We talked about how her difference makes her really special and unique. I saw something so special in Maya that day and it wasn't about how her body is different, it was the beautiful open loving heart inside of a girl that was being honest and hopeful about her challenges and life as a girl with a "super" leg!

Alana Nichols

ALANA NICHOLS is a three time Paralympic Gold medalist in the sports of Wheelchair Basketball and Alpine Skiing. She is the first female American to win gold medals in the summer and winter games and is passionately promoting the growth of adaptive surfing! Learn more at www.alanajanenichols.com.

Appendix: Resources

Below is a list of resources and links. Visit the websites to learn more about life-changing opportunities for individuals with physical disabilities. Individuals build confidence and gain inspiration to pursue their dreams. Go ahead, check out the Alpine ski and snowboarding, surfing, cycling, running, hockey, sailing, scuba diving, sailing, kayaking, rock climbing, water-skiing and whitewater rafting. Follow your dreams!

- Beckwith-Wiedemann Children's Foundation International (BWCFI), https://www.facebook.com/BWCFI/

- Alana Nichols, Ted Talks: Becoming the CEO of Yourself, http://www.alanajanenichols.com/all-about-alana/motivational-speaking.html

- National Sports Center for the Disabled (NSCD), http://nscd.org

- Stopbullying, https://www.stopbullying.gov.

- Snowbound, http://boundforsnow.com/meet-alana-nichols/

- Challenged Athletes Foundation (CAF), http://www.challengedathletes.org

- Junior Seau Foundation, Challenged Athletes Foundation (CAF), http://www.challengedathletes.org/junior-seau-adaptive-surfing-program-presented-caf/

- Adaptive Adventures, Colorado, https://adaptiveadventures.org.

About the Author

AT 10-YEARS OLD, Maya shares her unusual experiences and advice for kids who might be in similar situations. She continues her interest in writing, horse-back riding, sewing, bicycling, reading, hiking, swimming, and hanging out with her brothers...and her dog, Mango.

Maya spent the first 76 days of her life in the NICU and had three surgeries before she was 3-weeks old, plus other surgeries later. She has an uncommon toughness and a very pragmatic view of her life. Wise for her age, Maya does not define herself by her disability. She accepts her path and goes forward. She is a voice. She has lots to say. It seems that writing a book about her experience is a natural path for Maya. Who knows? Maybe after this, she might have more stuff to say. Connect with Maya at www.bubsmangomedia.com.

About the Illustrator

ROS WEBB is an Irish based artist who creates beautiful art blurring the line between fashion illustration and fine art. Ros has been featured in Vogue, Marie Claire and Elle Fashion magazines. Her art work is held in both private and public collections all over the world.

Ros Webb has been illustrating children's books for close to a decade and developed her own style as a children book artist following the birth of her first daughter and the publication of her picture book "The Big Sleepy Bear and the Pink Flamingos." Ros lives in the Irish mountains and is greatly inspired by her three children, fours dogs and four cats. She has worked extensively with authors from across the globe and is continually inspired by their imagination and story telling. Ros Webb now resides in West Cork, Ireland.

www.bubsmangomedia.com